SEVEN CANDLES FOR KWANZAA

Andrea Davis Pinkney ◆ *pictures by* Brian Pinkney

Dial Books for Young Readers ◆ New York

To Mom and Dad,
who've always taught me the importance of family.   A.D.P.

To my nieces, Gloria, Charnelle, and goddaughter, Victoria,
and to my nephew, Leon.   B.P.

Published by Dial Books for Young Readers · A Division of Penguin Books USA Inc.
375 Hudson Street · New York, New York 10014

Library of Congress Cataloging in Publication Data
Pinkney, Andrea Davis.
Seven candles for Kwanzaa / by Andrea Davis Pinkney ; pictures by Brian Pinkney.
p.   cm.
Summary: Describes the origins and practices of Kwanzaa, the seven-day festival
during which people of African descent rejoice in their ancestral values.
ISBN 0-8037-1292-8 (trade).—ISBN 0-8037-1293-6 (lib. bdg.)
1. Kwanzaa—Juvenile literature.
2. Afro-Americans—Social life and customs—Juvenile literature.
[1. Kwanzaa. 2. Afro-Americans—Social life and customs.]
I. Pinkney, J. Brian, ill. II. Title. III. Title: 7 candles for Kwanzaa.
GT4403.P56 1993   394.2'68—dc20   92-3698   CIP   AC

The full-color artwork was prepared using scratchboard, a technique that requires
a white board covered with black ink. The ink is then scraped off with a sharp tool
to reveal the white, which is painted over with oil pastels.

A Note to Readers

Kwanzaa is an American holiday inspired by African traditions. It is not intended as a religious, political, or heroic holiday, nor is it a substitute for Christmas. During the seven-day Kwanzaa festival, observed from December 26 through January 1, people of African descent rejoice in their ancestral values. A Swahili word, kwanza means "first." An extra "a" was added to the end of the word to give it seven letters, representing the holiday's seven principles. Kwanzaa's origins are in the agricultural harvest—or "first fruits"—celebrations that have been observed in countries throughout Africa for centuries. Many of these celebrations last seven days. Some occur in late December at the end of the year, and are celebrated until early January, the beginning of the next year. The dates for Kwanzaa correspond to the days of these African harvest festivals. Kwanzaa was created in 1966 by Maulana Karenga, Ph.D., chair and professor of Black Studies at the California State University at Long Beach, and executive director of the Institute of Pan-African Studies.

Seven principles are at the heart of Kwanzaa, and these are based on the gathering together of family, the commemoration of the ancestors, the rededication to the growth of the community, and the offering of gratitude for life's good. This book follows the sequence of Kwanzaa week and shows how its values may be expressed. Today millions of families in the United States celebrate the joys of Kwanzaa and look forward each year to a wonderful African-inspired celebration.

Kwanzaa (**kwahn**-zaah) is like a family day in the park and Thanksgiving and a birthday, all rolled into one! Kwanzaa is a joyous African-American holiday that is seven days long. It begins on December 26, and lasts through the first day of January.

The name *Kwanzaa* comes from the East African language of Swahili. It means first fruits of the harvest.

Since ancient times, in countries all over Africa, families have joined together to celebrate the end of the harvest and the beginning of the new planting season. When vegetables, yams, and fruits are ripe for gathering, families rejoice in a first fruits festival.

Kwanzaa is a holiday that began in America. It is a time when people whose ancestors come from Africa celebrate their African heritage. To get ready for the holiday, families decorate their homes with Kwanzaa symbols. They place the *mkeka* (em-**kay**-kah), a straw placemat, on a table. The mkeka is woven with beautiful patterns. It represents tradition.

Muhindi (moo-**hin**-dee) is corn. During Kwanzaa, one ear of corn is placed on the mkeka for each child in the family. Families that have many children put lots of muhindi on their mkeka—along with apples, bananas, nuts, pears, and yams—to remember the earth's abundance. These fruits and vegetables are called *mazao* (mah-**zah**-o), which means crops.

Kwanzaa gifts, made by hand, are called *zawadi* (zah-**wah**-dee). A fabric doll with black-button eyes, a necklace strung with speckled beads, and a homemade storybook with folktales from Africa are the kinds of zawadi that praise our African ancestry. Grown-ups give Kwanzaa gifts to children to reward them for the promises they've made and kept throughout the year. Children can give Kwanzaa gifts too.

Seven Kwanzaa candles are proudly placed in our *kinara* (kee-**nar**-rah), a wooden candle holder. A black candle in the center represents the richness of our skin. Three red candles are reminders of the struggles we sometimes have to face. Three green candles tell us to always look toward a prosperous future.

For each day of Kwanzaa one candle is lighted to celebrate a special principle. The seven Kwanzaa principles, called *Nguzo Saba* (en-**goo**-zo **sah**-bah), come from beliefs that are held by families in many parts of Africa. These beliefs help us learn, achieve, and grow.

On the first day of Kwanzaa the black candle is set alight to celebrate *umoja* (oo-**moe**-jah). The word *umoja* means unity. For umoja, our family gathers at home. We share thoughts and feelings about the Kwanzaa holiday, and relax in the spirit of togetherness. We talk, laugh, and ask *Habari gani* (hah-**bar**-ee **gah**-nee)?

Habari gani? is a Kwanzaa greeting that means What is the news? It is what we say to start each Kwanzaa day.

When someone asks Habari gani? we answer by telling about the Kwanzaa principle for that day.

If someone asks Habari gani? on the second day of Kwanzaa, the answer is *kujichagulia* (koo-jee-cha-goo-**lee**-ah), which means self-determination. A red candle is lit to represent kujichagulia. This is the day to learn traditions that help us define ourselves. In some families, women teach girls to braid their own hair in fancy styles. In others, folks learn to beat African rhythms on drums and gourds.

Habari gani?

What's the news on the third day of Kwanzaa? Collective work and responsibility, *ujima* (oo-**jee**-mah). Ujima is the Kwanzaa day to light a green candle and work together to get a family chore done, like stripping down an old wooden chair, and giving it a fresh coat of paint.

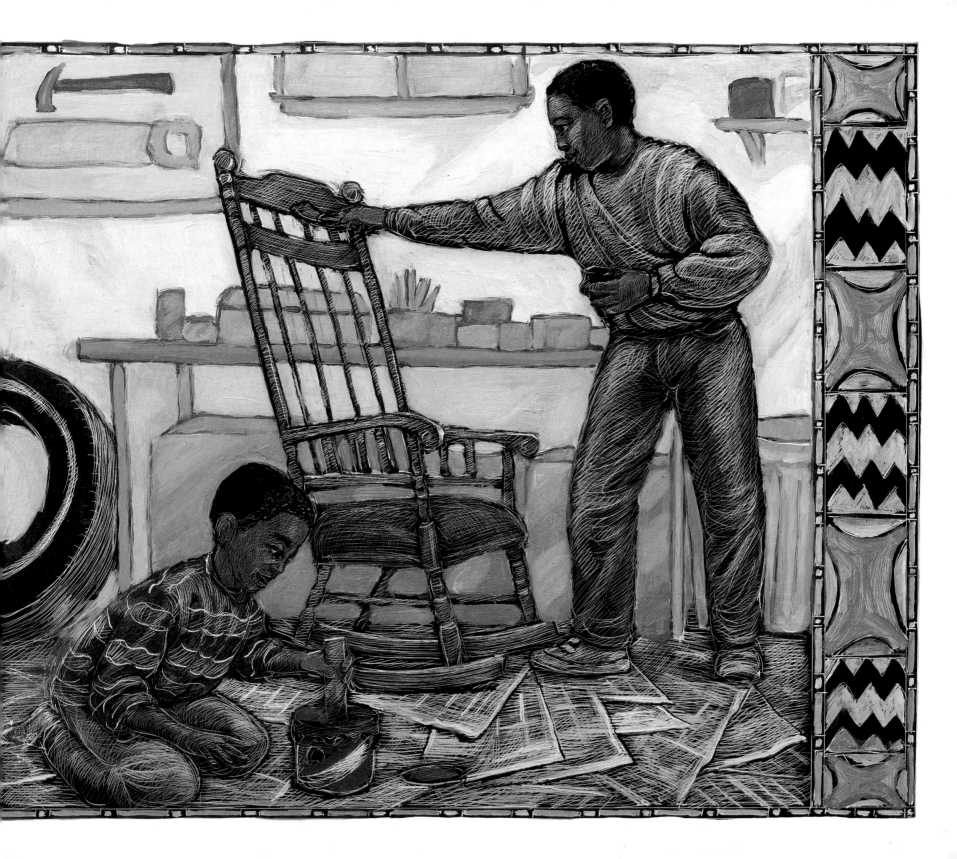

When the fourth day of Kwanzaa dawns, it's time to celebrate *ujamaa* (oo-jah-**maah**), cooperative economics. For ujamaa we save up our coins for one whole year to buy a family gift that everyone can share, like a clock that chimes, or a hallway mirror. On ujamaa day a red candle glows bright in the kinara.

Nia (**nee**-ah) is purpose, the fifth Kwanzaa principle. Today a second green candle glows to illuminate our purpose. This day of Kwanzaa is for reflecting on how to fill the days and years ahead. Some folks dream of life as an astronomer who peers at stars nestled in the dark night sky. Or a trumpet player who bebops in a swinging jazz band. Nia—our purpose—is to do what makes us glad to be who we are.

Kuumba (ku-**oom**-bah) means creativity, and the sixth day of Kwanzaa is for celebrating kuumba in every way. Today we make up dances to perform for friends. Some dances tell stories about the history of people who live in Africa. Other dances are just for fun.

Sculpting mounds of clay or reciting a favorite rhyme are also ways to express kuumba. So is planting seedlings on the windowsill and nurturing them to sprout. The third red candle shimmers to help our creativity shine.

Faith is *imani* (ee-**mahn**-ee), the seventh Kwanzaa principle. To have faith is to believe that good will always happen. To show our belief in a happy holiday, we burn the last green Kwanzaa candle. Our Kwanzaa *karamu* (kaa-**rah**-moo), a glorious feast, fills the room with the savory smells of roasted yams and collard greens.

To begin the karamu a grown-up spills a few drops of water from the *kikombe cha umoja* (kee-**kom**-bay cha oo-**moe**-jah), the family Kwanzaa cup. Each droplet honors our African ancestors. Everyone takes a little sip from the cup to drink in the warm feelings of family unity. Then all give thanks for our delicious food, and dig in to our Kwanzaa meal.

After dinner the party begins! The music sounds a soul-rousing rhythm. Everyone claps and shouts, rejoices and sings, and dances to celebrate a happy Kwanzaa.

Bibliography

Copage, Eric V. *Kwanzaa: An African-American Celebration of Culture and Cooking.* New York: William Morrow and Company, 1991.

Karenga, Maulana. *The African-American Holiday of Kwanzaa: A Celebration of Family, Community and Culture.* Los Angeles: University of Sankore Press, 1989.

Kifano, Subira. *Kwanzaa: A Special Holiday.* Los Angeles: University of Sankore Press, 1989.

McClester, Cedric. *Kwanzaa: Everything You Always Wanted to Know But Didn't Know Where to Ask.* New York: Gumbs & Thomas, Publishers, 1985.